O8-BCM-870

I0037949

Remember...
The best things in
life are free!

Titles by Marci
Published by
Blue Mountain Arts®

Friends Are Forever
A Gift of Inspirational Thoughts
to Thank You for Being
My Friend

10 Simple Things
to Remember
An Inspiring Guide to
Understanding Life

To My Daughter
Love and Encouragement
to Carry with You on Your
Journey Through Life

To My Mother
I Will Always Carry
Your Love in My Heart

To My Sister
A Gift of Love and Inspiration
to Thank You
for Being My Sister

You Are My "Once in a Lifetime"
I Will Always Love You

10

Simple Things to Remember

An Inspiring Guide to Understanding Life

Marci

Blue Mountain Press™
Boulder, Colorado

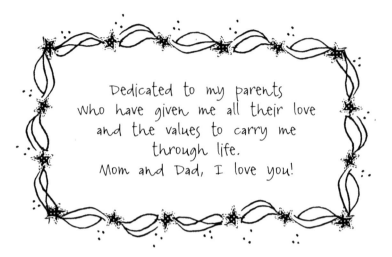

Dedicated to my parents
who have given me all their love
and the values to carry me
through life.
Mom and Dad, I love you!

Copyright © 2011 by Marci.

All rights reserved. No part of this publication may be reproduced, stored in a retrieval system or transmitted in any form or by any means, electronic, mechanical, photocopying, recording or otherwise, without the written permission of the publisher.

Library of Congress Control Number: 2011905028
ISBN: 978-1-59842-619-9

Children of the Inner Light is a registered trademark. Used under license.
Certain trademarks are used under license.

Printed in China.
Seventh Printing: 2014

 This book is printed on recycled paper.

This book is printed on paper that has been specially produced to be acid free (neutral pH) and contains no groundwood or unbleached pulp. It conforms with the requirements of the American National Standards Institute, Inc., so as to ensure that this book will last and be enjoyed by future generations.

Blue Mountain Arts, Inc.
P.O. Box 4549, Boulder, Colorado 80306

10 Simple Things to Remember

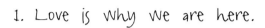

1. Love is why we are here.

2. The most important day is today.

3. If you always do your best, you will not have regrets.

4. In spite of your best efforts, some things are just out of your control.

5. Things will always look better tomorrow.

6. Sometimes a wrong turn will bring you to exactly the right place.

7. Sometimes when you think the answer is "no," it is just "not yet."

8. True friends share your joy, see the best in you, and support you through your challenges.

9. God and your parents will always love you.

10. For all your accomplishments, nothing will bring you more happiness than the love you find.

Introduction

This book first began as a greeting card of the same title. When I wrote it, my intention was to simplify important concepts, along with a philosophy for living, into ten easy-to-understand thoughts that when absorbed together gave the reader a sense that the ideas I expressed could be applied to almost any life situation. The greeting card is one of my own personal favorites. The writing of this book told me why.

I realized I had laid in front of me ten chapters, each representative of the beliefs, philosophies, and strategies to cope with life that I hold dear. I brought to mind my own personal journey, recalling the ups, the downs, and the lessons learned. And as I finished the book, I realized I had a gift of what I believe ready to pass on to those I love.

For as long as I can remember, I have been on a quest to understand this great miracle that is our story. When I started, I thought that understanding life would make living it easier... What I found was that life is a mystery we may never fully understand and that the path to serenity comes through acceptance.

For most of us, life is difficult no matter how much we try to understand it because of the inevitable challenges that come our way in the form of relationship struggles, accidents, illnesses, and the loss of loved ones. But we can learn ways to cope... And more importantly, we can recognize the opportunities for spiritual growth that our struggles offer us.

We can choose to connect with others in a way that makes us feel whole... We can evaluate our beliefs and our values and integrate these into our daily lives through our actions... And we can understand life as a "call to love" and, through our efforts, live in a better world.

Enjoy!

Marci

Hope

1

Love
is why
we are here.

It is only natural to wonder about the meaning of life. Since man has been able to question, he has asked: "Why are we here?" "What is the purpose of life?" and "Where do I fit in?" Volumes have been written on the subject — in hopes of answering what seems to be a question built into mankind — as we hunger to learn about the mysteries of life. Remember... love is the greatest force on earth, and it is why we are here.

Love Is...

Love is a verb. Love is not just a feeling; it is an action. It is most evident in what you do, for there will be days when you will be called to love even when you may not have feelings of love.

Love is a choice. Understanding this concept will change your life significantly and may determine your ability to maintain lifelong happiness.

Love never ends. The greatest gift you can give to yourself or another is the gift of commitment... to say "I do" but also "I will."

Love is giving all you have and asking for little in return. It is sharing the joys, but also supporting another through sorrow and spiritual growth.

Love is forgiving. Only God can love you unconditionally... the rest of us are human. Do not ask for perfection from others, because they will make mistakes. Forgive easily, and challenge only yourself to understand what it means to love unconditionally. Do not ask how others can love you more → ask how you can love them more. You will be blessed with the understanding that the bonds we have are as everlasting as the spirit.

Learn About Love...

The journey of life gives us many opportunities to learn about love. Our births begin our quest for "home." Our mothers are the very first people to love us, so our understanding of love in the beginning is limited to our needs. As we continue along the path of life, we may have siblings, and later we have friends. These relationships give us expanding ways to understand what it means to give and receive... to understand and be understood... and to connect with another human being in a way that gives life meaning. As we mature, our relationships, including our friendships, become more important. They give us significant insights into ourselves as we test the waters, learning about relationships and experiencing what it really means "to love."

Love is not a feeling — love is an action... love is a choice.

The happiest moments in life take place in the context of relationships.

If you want to experience unconditional love, do not put conditions on it.

Say "I Love You" Every Day

If you are in need of a gift for a loved one, write a love letter — tell them what they have meant in your life.

Spend time with your spouse — just holding hands.

When you're tempted to say one more thing — let it be "I love you."

There are three
things that last...
faith, hope, and love.

Once in a lifetime someone
comes into your life that you
really connect with heart to
heart... soul to soul.
A friendship develops and
love follows.

To love and be loved... that is
life's greatest gift. To share joy
with those most important in
our lives... that is a blessing.

2

The most
important day
is today.

Life is difficult. This is a fact. Life is busy... and this can be something that we can't change as much as we want to. We try to juggle so many different things, wanting to give a piece of ourselves to our jobs, our friends, our families, and the people we share our lives with. We can be left with a sense that we will never catch up, and we wonder if we will be able to find time for ourselves. This is a time to remember... the most important day is today.

Focus on Today

Yesterday is gone... tomorrow only exists in the future. These, of course, are facts, but they are easy to forget as we spend so much precious energy thinking about things we did or didn't do... or worrying about what might happen tomorrow.

Age-old wisdom tells us that serenity is a state of being in which happiness is achieved by being fully and only aware of the moment. This is not a state of doing, but rather of experiencing one's existence with gratitude. We might wonder how to achieve this mysterious state in our ever-busier world.

The trick is to be fully conscious of our thoughts, to remember the simple things, to take time to stop and say "thank you" for little treasures like a gentle breeze...
dropping rain...
birds chirping...
leaves rustling in the wind...
the smell of honeysuckle...
freshly cut grass...
a baby's laughter...
a smile...
a hug.
Life is so much better when we enjoy the perfect moment of now.

Don't Worry

There are two days in the
week that are not important...
yesterday and tomorrow.
Focus on today.

Don't forget to have fun.

Sometimes a good laugh
is all you need.

Whatever is happening in your life,
keep these things in mind:

Big problems can be solved in small steps.

When you are still, the gentle voice from
within will guide you... listen carefully.

Remember to pray, and let God take
the burden of worry from your heart.

Accept that we each learn life's lessons
in our own way.

A lot of people love you more than
words can say.

Today Is a Gift...

Gratitude is one of life's greatest gifts, and it is free for the choosing. When we make this choice, we are demonstrating an understanding of our free will.

Gratitude is a practice... an exercise in which we train our minds to look at the good things before us each day, no matter what is happening in our lives.

Gratitude is a state of mind we cultivate in ourselves that enables us to understand that often it is our greatest challenges and losses that bring us our greatest lessons.

Gratitude is the place from which we recognize life's compensations that are always before us, so we can enjoy each day with thanksgiving.

This is a day to look forward...
but also a day to look back... to
see what has brought us here and
to give thanks for all that has
happened on the road of life. It
is the love and joy we attain that
warms our lives and our hearts, but
it is the challenges we overcome
that allow us to truly feel the
glow of accomplishment.
Celebrate the future...
Hold dear the past...
and remember that "today" is the
greatest gift of all!

3

If you always do your best, you will not have regrets.

Everyone has dreams... Often we wonder, "Just how do we attain them?" We might have an idea... and we might try to work out every detail and solve every problem before we decide to move forward. But what we often find is that we never feel secure enough to take the leap! We worry about mistakes, causing us to think and think about what we want, while our dreams become locked in our imaginations. So how do we move our dreams out of our heads and onto the path of success? When you wonder how to get closer to your dreams, remember... if you always do your best, you will not have regrets.

choose Your Path

The path to one's dreams is filled with choices... little packages along the way that we open as we go. Sometimes we make the right choice, and this moves us forward. Sometimes we make a mistake, and it puts us three steps back. And sometimes we make what we thought was a wrong choice only to find out later that this package was a gift after all!

The most important thing is that through the process some call "the game of life," you always strive to do your best. When you come from this place known as "intention," your dreams begin to unfold before you. Possibilities you never imagined appear, and because you are sharing your best self, you are shown the gifts you have to share. When you learn to accept all that has happened along the way as necessary for your understanding, you will be able to view your life without regrets.

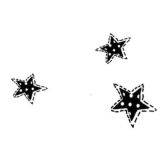

FAITH
HOPE
LOVE

Accept All That Has Happened

If you have learned something from every experience, there should be no regrets. If you understand that learning is a process, there are no wrong decisions.

Making mistakes is a very important part of life... It's the foundation for empathy toward your fellow man.

Everything always works out as it should, though often it's just not what you had in mind.

Wisdom comes with experience;
it's usually the painful events
that hold the greatest lessons.

Life is a process, not an event.
All that you experience is necessary
for your understanding.

Fighting against the way things are
causes most personal suffering —
acceptance is the path to serenity.
One of life's paradoxes:
acceptance creates the fertile
soil for change.

Share Your Best Self...

Virtues are the steppingstones by which we get to our dreams. They are references to live by. They are truths held in high esteem by sages since the beginning of time. It might be accurate to say that every great religion and every respected philosopher will agree to the importance these qualities play in enriching our lives.

By tapping into the part of ourselves that is whole and good, we find a treasure chest of feelings that rewards us with the understanding of the essence of the human spirit.

Sharing is one of these virtues. When we share "things," we divide limited resources... but when we share ourselves, we tap into the gifts within to find a renewable source of energy called love.

When we get in touch with our "inner light," we discover that which is known as "our best selves." When we share this part of our being, we feel the most authentic. We have a sense about our worth and our place in the universe.

We learn what our strengths are. We open ourselves to those who have complementary gifts. We respect all contributions as equal and necessary in the grand scheme. We find joy in the accomplishments of others, and through this process of connecting, our path in life becomes clear.

4

In spite of your best efforts, some things are just out of your control.

Great teachers in both the present and the past all seem to agree that the key to our well-being lies in experiencing the joy found in the present moment. Yet we struggle when things go wrong, wondering if we could have done this or that to make a difference. We second-guess decisions we made... "holding on" when we should be "letting go." This kind of thinking spends precious energy trying to change things that cannot be changed, and it keeps us from enjoying the good things that are in our lives now. At these times, remember... in spite of your best efforts, some things are just out of your control.

Everything Happens for a Reason

So often we wonder about the "whys" in life... "Why did this happen?" "Why me?" "Why now?" But there is a secret that wise people know...

Bumps in the road are an inevitable part of life that soften us, make us grow, and bestow upon us the virtue of compassion. Often, it is only with the passing of time that it becomes clear the cloud really did have a silver lining, and now we have wisdom, strength, and hope to share. And at last, we understand the true meaning of the phrase...

"Everything happens for a reason."

No matter where life takes you or what path you choose, you will always meet challenges. That is the way life is. There are no guarantees, and no matter how many things you do right or how many rules you follow, there will always be that fork in the road that makes you choose between this way or that. Whenever you meet this place, remember these things: You are loved... love will sustain you. You are strong... prayer will get you through anything. You are wise... the greatest gift of all lies within you.

Learn to Let Go

It can be unsettling to admit how little control over our lives we really have. So many life-changing events just happen. People leave us, hurt us, and sometimes get sick. The forces of nature can destroy our homes and all that we have worked so hard for, causing what seems like unexplained suffering. Our bodies get older and can let us down. Accidents can change our lives in ways that are irreversible, and we can be left asking, "What do we have control of?" These are times to remember that our struggles are opportunities to give and receive love. When we say "thank you" for the gift of life in the face of hardship, we demonstrate our ability to choose the way we see things. When we make this choice, we are on our way to understanding what we really have control of in this life... and that is our actions.

Most things in life we have no control over — but we do have a choice about how we see them.

Roadblocks are obstacles that push us back on track. Focusing inward on our own choices, instead of trying to move mountains, frees up energy that turns roadblocks into steppingstones.

Do the best you can with what you know today, and always be willing to learn.

Let go of the past. Take responsibility for the facts of your life... Move forward.

There Is a Greater Plan

Write down your dream and tuck it away — entrusting that all things will come at the right time.

Life is that dance we do in the space between "making it happen" and "letting it happen."

Think about the big picture; let go of the details. Intention is powerful.

Close your eyes and envision
the source of

all that is love...
   all that is good...
      all that is whole...

shining on you with a gentle
but all-powerful light,
bringing healing,
comfort,
hope,
and wellness...
Experience the magnificent,
all-healing power of God!

5

Things will always look better tomorrow.

Happiness is a state of mind that we all want to use to describe our lives. How can we feel successful at all if we cannot say we are happy? What good is money and family and the love that we give and receive if we do not perceive ourselves as happy? Many times we feel that we have little control over our circumstances, and we are left dependent on forces outside ourselves in order to experience happiness. Most of us believe that our state of mind depends on what is around us. But when we observe life and people who have survived losses and tragedies, we begin to realize that something important is at work "inside" these individuals... It is the life-changing concept that we can actually choose to be happy. Remember... things will always look better tomorrow.

Stay Positive...

Hope is an attitude. It is a mental shift that we choose for ourselves as we tap into our inner reserves. When we decide to be hopeful, we open ourselves to discover the wisdom and strength we may not have known existed. When we ask ourselves to stay positive and we answer the call, we are rewarded with the knowledge of what we have learned in life. Our lessons, when viewed from this perspective, show us that things generally work out as they should. With hindsight, we are able to understand how a greater plan has been working in our lives.

Hope is a gift we can give to others as we encourage their dreams, comfort their sorrows, and remind them that miracles are before us every day.

Often, we never know just how much it meant to give courage to another, but soon we realize that this gift is one of the simple free things in life that we can rely on — no matter what is happening in our lives or in the lives of those we care about.

Hope is transforming. It becomes an act of love when we extend ourselves for our own spiritual growth or for that of another... and like love, hope always comes full circle to renew the spirit. We are given a glimpse of our true nature and rewarded with the wonderful treasure found in our connections with others.

Remain Hopeful

If you have faith, hope, love, and the blessing of good friends, you will get through whatever challenges life brings. Your faith will light your path... hope will keep you strong... the love you give to others will bring you joy... and your friendships will remind you of what is important in life.

Give thanks for each day in advance.

Hope

After a big storm —
look for a rainbow.

Help is always there
when you are ready.

Sometimes you may feel that you
are all alone, as life brings
challenges to overcome and
hardships to bear. But when you
least expect it, help will appear.

Change Your Mind, Change Your Life

There are times in our lives when happiness seems to elude us. We want more... We wish we were further along in our lives... We desire better relationships... We try to push ourselves beyond where we are at the moment. Sometimes, all that is needed is a change of mind... a change called "acceptance." With this change comes a sense of peace and a sudden realization that a "shift in thinking" has brought us the very things we were looking for all along.

On the days when things get difficult, remember it is perseverance that will get you through. Give thanks for the talent that has set you on your path, for the inner strength that has helped you navigate the obstacles, and for the faith that has carried you through the most difficult of days! You will succeed! Hang in there! You can do it!

Follow Your Dreams

6

Sometimes a wrong turn will bring you to exactly the right place.

Life is a journey. One that we essentially have to take alone. Yes, we have parents to guide us and sometimes siblings to forge the way. We have friends to walk by our sides and teachers and people we admire to mentor us, but in the final analysis, we choose our paths ourselves... and we do it one step at a time through the many choices we make. We sense we are going blindly along... waiting for the day when we know the secrets the universe holds. We listen for our calling, believing that this voice will show us the way. Sometimes while traveling a road we think is just right, we discover an exciting adventure right in our path that we had never even considered. Remember... sometimes a wrong turn will bring you to exactly the right place.

All Paths Lead to Home...

If only we had a road map to take us through life — a guidebook presented to us at birth that would show us the way home. Maybe we do! And part of the excitement in life is found in learning to pay attention to all the little signs along the way that point to "this way" or "that." Sometimes when we are searching for an answer, a total stranger may have what we need. Sometimes when we need a friendly ear to listen as we work out a problem, the phone rings and brings us a friend! And sometimes information we are looking for just shows up on a sign along the road! Have fun as you watch your story being written, and remember... angels are everywhere!

51

Just Believe

Sometimes our lives take a turn that we never expected and we are faced with the challenge to begin anew. We can feel overwhelmed and wonder if we will ever get through this day, much less the days ahead. Remember to take it one day at a time, accepting each day with courage and faith.

Soon you may discover that a "new beginning" has opened a door that you never imagined and has shown you another path to take you home!

Faith Is the Way

We don't always get what we want...
but we always get what we need.

Live each day open to guidance, and
your path in life will become clear.

All Paths Lead
to Home

Holding on to the familiar is comforting, but life does not stand still and it does not look back. There are only a few certainties in life, and one of those is that there will always be change. Remember, as you move forward to accept each day as it comes, consider the possibility that "change is good."

The road of life has many turns...
sometimes taking us to a place we
had planned... sometimes showing us
a surprise around the bend we could
never have anticipated. We make
decisions based on the information we
have... We accept the ups and downs
as they come... We live "one day at
a time"... but often we find it is
only when we look back that we
can see that what we thought was
a "wrong turn" has brought us to
exactly the right place and every
step was a right one after all!

7

Sometimes when you think the answer is "no," it is just "not yet."

As we travel this mysterious journey known as "our life," we often feel a tug to move. We try to respond... searching, like Dorothy did for Oz, for the rainbow that is our dream. We might begin, thinking we know the way to go, only to find an obstacle in our path that keeps us from moving forward. We make the best decisions we can with the information we have at the time. But we forget that there is an order to the universe, and sometimes in spite of our best efforts, we do not get what we wanted. We forget that there is a greater plan, laid by the Master Designer... one in which our needs are always taken care of... and in perfect timing. Remember... sometimes when you think the answer is "no," it is just "not yet."

All Things Will Come in the Right Time

There is a right time for everything. The universe teaches us this important concept with its order. There is a sunrise and sunset... Days turn into weeks, and weeks into months... There are tides that ebb and flow with a rhythm and timing written long ago... And so it is with our lives.

There is a greater plan at work... one that is set into motion when we are born. As we navigate the journey called "life," we begin the work of discovering "who we are." This is primarily a process of defining what we believe.

Much of this work takes place in
the context of our relationships as
we learn from our choices and
experience all the feelings
associated with love —
love for family...
love for friends...
and love for someone we hope
to be with forever.

There It Is
in
Black + White

Some of the most important ways we define ourselves come from the obstacles we face, the challenges we overcome, and the losses we sustain, as it is most often the difficult times in our lives that call us to understand what we are made of.

Knowing what we believe is critical to our serenity and sense of happiness, because every decision we make in our lives will ultimately come down to using this self-knowledge as a frame of reference.

Making decisions that match our beliefs is the essence of living with integrity and provides us with a sense of wholeness.

It is often this work of self-discovery that needs to be progressed to a certain place before the universe is ready to show us our life's purpose.

Your life holds for you endless possibilities. You have built a solid foundation, and you have worked hard for it. Continue to do what is necessary to move forward one day at a time. Keep sight always of what is important in life. Live each day open to guidance, and your purpose will be revealed to you. Your future is filled with love and acceptance.

True happiness and purpose will be found in relationships with each other and with God. It is often through sharing your gifts and talents that your path in life will become clear. It is when you are "giving" that others can see in you that which is known as "your best self." Pray, be open to guidance, and remember: God takes care of your dreams.

8

True friends share your joy, see the best in you, and support you through your challenges.

Everyone has the desire to love and be loved... to understand and be understood. This need, basic to human nature, is fulfilled through friendship. We experience the emotions that bring deep gratification by opening ourselves to others and, most importantly, by creating the trust necessary for others to open themselves to us. Friendship is such an important gift because it is a path to understanding the age-old question, "Why are we here?" It also allows us to understand who we are as we see our best selves reflected in the eyes of a friend. When you think about friendship, remember... true friends share your joy, see the best in you, and support you through your challenges.

Be a Good Friend

Friendship is a gift of commitment. It lives up to the expectation that each partner is there for the other through the ups and downs of life.

Friendship is a gift of trust. There is an understanding that with the exchange of hopes, dreams, joys, sorrows, and secrets, one can count on the other to keep a confidence.

Friendship is a gift of listening. It resists the temptation to give solutions to problems, and it understands that silent listening is one of the greatest acts of unconditional love.

Friendship is a gift of encouragement. It freely offers the inspiration needed to remain courageous in the face of life's daily challenges.

Friendship means never having to face the challenges of life alone.

Friendship means sharing a closeness of spirit that gives life meaning.

Friendship means having a witness to life's tiny, special moments that are so much better when shared.

Friendship means that there is someone who understands where you've been, knows where you want to go, and accepts you for who you are.

Friendship Is a Gift...

Friendship is one of our most valuable gifts. It completes our desire to realize our capacity to love. It brings to our lives that closeness that makes us feel connected and whole and that lets us know we are not alone in the world.

Friendship fills the universal need to share, and at the same time, it gives us a glimpse of our own true nature. The exchanges of the heart that happen between friends create memories that last a lifetime, and those memories become treasures that warm us on the coldest of days.

As we share our thoughts, fears, hopes, and dreams with another through friendship, we are given the opportunity to really understand just how alike we are. When we support each other through life's challenges, we are shown that we have so much love to give.

Cherish your friends...
remember your lives were
brought together for a reason.

Friends can do
anything or nothing
and have the best time.

A good friend
is always ready to listen.

Sometimes, All You Need Is a Hug

Friendship grows on exchanges of the heart!

A good friendship brightens every day!

A Hug Is Worth a Thousand Words!

Friends share life's most precious memories!

If you have good friends... you have almost everything!

9

God and
your parents
will always
love you.

There are times in our lives when life is difficult... things don't work out as planned... or a special relationship is strained. We feel a loss or sadness, and we think that no one could possibly understand what we are going through. We may be battling an illness... or someone we love is struggling. There is a sense of loneliness, and we long to feel a part of something good and whole. This is a time to hold on to love and remember... God and your parents will always love you.

Love Will
Get You Through...

Love is a miracle. It has given poets
and authors reason to write for thousands
of years.
We ponder its meaning...
We seek its light...
We experience joy because of it...
We grieve at its loss...
And we stand in awe of its power.

Great novels have tales of love woven
through their pages, drawing us in, like
the aroma of baking bread to a bakery.
We must go.
We sense that love will fill us up...
wake us up... and answer every question
we have about life.
And we are right!

Love, as much as we try to define it,
only holds up to its definition as a verb.
When we commit ourselves and say, "I
will," we begin to understand the
mysterious, life-sustaining miracle called love.

A Parent's Love
Is Everlasting

Children know and adults remember that the fun, the love, and the bonds we make are as everlasting as the spirit.

Love is powerful and gentle at the same time.

When parents live as they believe, they give their children a gift that lasts a lifetime.

A mother's love is a blessing that will be always in your heart.

A father's love is a gift that lasts forever.

Love from a Parent

You are always in my heart
and never far from my thoughts,
because on the day you were born,
I promised to love you forever.
My wish is that you find a place
in the world that gives you a sense
of contribution...
that you find the kind of love
that makes the stars shine brighter...
and that you know the gift of
gratitude that comes with living
a life of compassion.
Remember,
wherever you are,
whatever you do,
wherever life takes you,
I will always love you.

God's Love Has No End

You are my child and my finest creation. I made you in my image and likeness so you would know that you are whole. When you look inside in the place that is your spirit, you will find pure love and know that I will be with you forever.
My wish is that you understand that love is why you are here...
that you accept all that has happened along your journey as lessons...
that you learn that gratitude and compassion are your gifts to receive.
In all ways remember,
wherever you are,
whatever you do,
wherever you choose to go in life,
I will be with you until the end of time.

God Is Love

Give to others the very things you most need... support, encouragement, and hope. Giving always goes in a circle and returns to renew the spirit.

Open your heart to the grace of God through prayer. When you ask for help, you create within yourself the conditions to receive God's love.

Do the best you can for today. Do not ask more of yourself than you can handle today. You are a child of God, and you will be cared for in a way you may only understand tomorrow.

Angels Are Everywhere

Sometimes we feel that we are all alone, as life brings us challenges to overcome and hardships to bear. But when we least expect it, help can appear. It may be a kind word from a stranger or a phone call at just the right time, and we are suddenly surrounded with the loving grace of God. Miracles happen every day because angels are everywhere.

10

For all your accomplishments, nothing will bring you more happiness than the love you find.

When we are young, ideas form in our minds about what life will be... what is important... and what will bring us happiness. We set goals for ourselves and work hard to achieve them. We go to school, feel accomplished when we get good grades, and begin to learn about relationships. Our parents and our families are our first experience in seeing ourselves through the eyes of another, but as we venture out into the world and gain experience, our friendships take on greater importance. One day we fall in love... As life continues, we may have children and discover a whole new kind of love that surprises us with its intensity. One day we realize that love gives us a yardstick by which we can measure things that are meaningful, and we can put in order the things that are really important. Remember... for all your accomplishments, nothing will bring you more happiness than the love you find.

Hold On to Love...

We learn about life through trial and error. From an early age we begin to formulate in our minds what we will be when we are grown. The idea that being accomplished in our chosen profession will bring us happiness is communicated to us in an unconscious way. Some people spend all their lives working, only to find themselves feeling that something is missing.

The challenges of life often push us to reevaluate what we believe. Our relationships ask us to be all that we can be; they show us our strengths and our weaknesses. They also give us the place to experience what the wise and the elderly all agree is a fundamental truth, and that is... "Love is why we are here after all!"

Life's greatest purpose can
be found in relationships.

Success is empty without people
you love to share it with.

When you share joy, it multiplies.
When you share pain, it divides.

It is our connections with our
parents, our children, our spouses,
and our friends that provide us
with everlasting joy.

Be Happy

The quest for happiness is the plot line for everyone's story. Happiness is the pot of gold at the end of the rainbow... It is the place called "Oz" that one finally reaches when following the yellow brick road... It is the universal desire that gives us a sense of completeness when we can say that we are happy.

We might wonder how to achieve this elusive state of being, especially in today's world where the advances we've made in technology have not rewarded us with more time, but instead have asked us to do more of everything and do it faster! We thought the advances of this new era would offer us a new path to happiness, but instead we are left feeling as though we can never catch up with our lives.

While it may be true that our discoveries have given us more choices and new ways to communicate, the question poses itself: Do the strides made in technology, science, and medicine enhance our ability to realize serenity and experience unconditional love? We know we cannot say "yes" to this question, because in truth, the same basic things that every generation can attest to are what bring us fulfillment.

So how do we get back to these things and to the place where we remember that everything we need in our lives is always and already there?

All we need are simple tools... Keys that help us unlock the secrets that enable us to experience ourselves as happy. These Keys are things we can remember... attitudes we can take... and, most importantly, choices we can make in our daily lives that make a difference.

First, we can realize that happiness is a choice... we can make the decision to "be happy" each day. We can accept what may seem like a revolutionary idea that we actually have a choice about seeing our lives as happy... and that our state of mind need not depend entirely on circumstances around us.

We can remember that happiness is found somewhere "inside" of ourselves — when we look within, we find the gifts that we have to share. In doing so, we make someone smile, and the good feelings return to renew the spirit.

We can adopt an attitude of gratefulness. We can remember that the most precious things in life are the things that were free all along... There is the love that we give and receive... and the joy that we experience and share... but there are also the sorrows and heartaches, which are an inevitable part of our human existence, that enrich our experience in ways we are not prone to acknowledge...

Our losses and the pain we feel give us a yardstick by which we can measure our happiness. The challenges we face, which often include our own shortcomings, make us more compassionate human beings as our understanding of others is broadened.

When we reach this place of acceptance and experience what it really means to have a grateful heart, we live each day with the understanding that everything happens for a reason.

We can give something beautiful and free to another... encouragement. When we inspire another through simple kindness and positive words, we find that we have discovered what we were looking for all along — an unending source of a beautiful gift called happiness!

Love has no end.

About Marci

Marci began her career by hand painting floral designs on clothing. No one was more surprised than she was when one day, in a single burst of inspiration and a completely new and different art style, her delightful characters sprang from her pen! "Their wild and crazy hair is a sign of strength," she thought, "and their crooked little smiles are endearing." She quickly identified the charming characters as Mother, Daughter, Sister, Father, Son, Friend, and so on until all the people and places in life were filled. Then, with her own loved ones in mind, she wrote a true and special sentiment to each one. This would be the beginning of a wonderful success story, which today still finds Marci writing each and every one of her verses in this same personal way.

Marci is a self-taught artist who has always enjoyed writing and art. She is thrilled to see how her delightful characters and universal messages of love have touched the hearts and lives of people everywhere. Her distinctive designs can also be found on Blue Mountain Arts greeting cards, calendars, bookmarks, and other gift items.

To learn more about Marci, look for Children of the Inner Light on Facebook or visit her website: www.MARCIonline.com.